CROWN POINT
& OTHER POEMS

Acknowledgements to *Bim*, *Kyk-over-Al*, *Caribbean Quarterly*, *Trinidad and Tobago Review*, *Arts Review*, *Focus*, *Pathways*, and to Heinemann (*Jamaica Woman*) all of which have published some of these poems.

CROWN POINT
& OTHER POEMS

VELMA POLLARD

PEEPAL TREE

First published in Great Britain in 1988
Reprinted in 2003
Peepal Tree Press Ltd
17 King's Avenue
Leeds LS6 1QS
England
Reprinted 2003

ISBN 0 948833 24 6

CONTENTS

To my children
Michele, Michael and Brian

and in memory of my grandmother
Eva Elizabeth Harris

CROWN POINT

The sea hums endlessly
Stars through the darkness
wake my hupentery peace...

'...A see mi great granfather
jumping hopscotch and playing marble...'

I see MY grandmother praying

'...Bless the Lord oh my soul
and all that is within me
bless his holy name...'

and the round green world of penny-royal smells the room
through windows cool and sweet
And khus-khus from the cupboard counter-smells.

On the shelf her pan
a miniature suitcase black and red
with stamps and old receipts and dust
there too her bible large and black
its file of leaves in red
turned to us kneeling
this bible full...
God's words and other words
birth dates and marriages
and deaths

'... and forget not all his benefits
who forgiveth all thy iniquities
who healeth all thy diseases
who satisfieth thy mouth with good things...'

Thus speaks my Gran
through this Tobago silence...
and recreates the order of her room
and recreates the aura of her God
and speaks so clearly in me...

Perhaps the clutter of my life
obscures her voice
Perhaps the clutter of my mind
frustrates her
streaming to my consciousness
Perhaps her mystic to me
waits my silence
waits my tomorrows' spaces.

RAIN THOUGHTS

raindrops fall soft on city eaves.
at home
small men
their trousers rolled knee-high
their half felt-hats pulled down
hold firm banana leaves
umbrellas long and green
mocking the rain...
and to their cows and goats
(who like the rain
no more than humans do)
rush uncomplaining

and women
large
bandanad
many-skirted
check their load
wrapped and re-wrapped
in quail banana leaves
brown plastic leading off the rain

and barefoot children
giggle sidewalk gutters
whitening their toes
against the tiny tide
come rippling down the stones
raindrops fall soft...

KINGSTON

moonshine baby
ring time
rain showers
play time
set out your fingers
set out your toes
daliman daliman
daliman one...

But here there are no children
for pint-sized scrunters
walk the endless plazas
whispering their pleas
'gimme a ten cents no'
and pint-sized sufferers
haunt traffic lights
unsummoned
to your wind-screen

no mothers for moonshine
no grannies warming loving cans
with mint or black-sage
sweet and hot
sound sleep and peaceful dreams
and early morning rising
dew will clear your eyes
the mist bring strength

This tractless city
withering the young
old people festering in the slums
hope felt now hopeless
darkness down-
pressing

till the mind forgets
its country moonshines
with their dreams
of city streets alive...

stark now
and stinking
with the stench
of dead hopes
rotting.

YALLER/YELLOW

Negro children
saucer eyes
mango skin
mango hair
shouting in fear
'go weh, yu black!'

shame shame black Mamma
sit and teach
your yellow children
truth shines out
their negro lips
their saucer eyes

or will you wait
till further north
some white child tells them
'black stand back'?

HOPE
(For Joyce and Howard 1978)

Then
there was green hope
leaves bringing life
then young sap sprung
sure that bark would live

Now
young men package grand-
mothers trudging blood-
spattered feet to tell
the king they come
guardians of all things
bright bearing arms

No customs
raise no fingers pointing loud
no voice forbids their haste
and great grandmother's spirit
flits around
blessing the time
that called her home

this shameless change
so soon these leaves
dry crackle underfoot
parched earth peers up
to brittle bark
to leafless branch

But the desert stalk will stand
the cactus with its bright red
bristling at the tip
roses need not be red
nor leaves midribbed
in one eternal tidiness

some tiny shrublets
hold their blooms
nor every sunset fade
Believer look
touch now their gentler shape
and in their beauty
Hope embrace.

NATIONAL HEROES 1980

How many Baptist heads must young Salome seek
because she danced the Horah for a king?

how many times must tumbrils
rumbling pass from lady Guillotine?

how many Jewless houses Hitler do you ask?

how many Blacks must dot the middle stream?

how many corpses dangling in the wind
must feed their stench
must poison all this land
before you retributive givers
cancelling plagues
call off your hounds of hell?

SUNDAY THOUGHTS
(FRENCHMAN'S COVE)

Troubled with ologies
the paper tigers claw us and each other
raking the muck that smells in tier on tier
poisoning the land

but in the cove where almond trees
orelias and their parasites hang cool
where blue/green
gently hugs thejutting rock-face
every second splash
or lover-rough and hungry
hurls whiteness on its grey
calm holds the earth

beyond
space hides the ripples
blue/green marble
stretches to a boundless edge
unless a smart canoist
sudden turns his boat
and somehow marks
that something ends here
or begins

that smooth sea
hides the litter of a thousand earths
washed in by earthquake storm or tidal wave
perhaps
the sea will wash our land
perhaps
destruction with its blessed cleansing
will call our country
to a baptism.

FISHERMAN

Fisherman
you know your net
you know the ill-starred puffed-up fish
who swims with confidence
flexing his fins

Smile Walrus fisherman
and weep with motions
casting out your net
spreading its glassy weave
and waiting, waiting patiently
till flexed fins rest
till confidence relaxes on the weave

then watch your hapless catch
squirm on the wooden surface
of your quaint canoe
its fish eyes crazed in wonder
So many many ill-starred mates

BUD/UNBUDDED

This bud beheld me watch
her glory folded
This bud beheld me move one minute spot in time
Unbudded/Outrose/her petals myriading...

This flower sees me watch
her glory flaunted
This flower hears me pause and knows I pause
to grieve for her tomorrows spaces.

BIRD KISS

blue grey
my bright noon sky
twin birds
identical from here
and black
rush to each other
clutch
then quickly disengage

quick kiss
beneath the feathers
in the high noon sun?
quick snarl beneath the feathers
in the harsh noon sun?

I favour love
black boy black girl
bird kiss me quick
then laughing wing vault
through the blue grey sky

FROM SENIOR'S AT GORDON TOWN

grass rippling
upward
like young smoke rising
like silver foam
sun-edge on water

textures
are hard to catch
on paper

light crawls
upslope
and trees stand silent
wind grass
lapping at their feet
to ripple up
then down that other side
touching a silver sky

MOONIIOPE

Casuarinas brush
the edge of moon
and click their lenses
now before the deep
blue tinged with orange
nightmare shroud
cloud masks her

But soon
the moon her light
confounds the blue
scatters the orange
blazes forth
untinged by blue
untinged by orange now

Now casuarinas
gaze their wonder
climbing at the moon
her graceful distancing
and casuarinas wait
to catch
that shining edge... tomorrow

A CASE FOR PAUSE

Arrest the sense
and let the fancy flow
Without design
collecting cloud and air
petal and leaf...

Rein in the fancy now
unleash the sense...
constructs and theories
not yet pursued
rush in perfected, whole

Each pausing briefly rests
to rising work its best
shadows and moonlight
dust and then the rain
each dies the while
to brightly live again

MOODS

I

Night

The trombone's last note
dies; the drum's timpano trembles;
the drummer's hand
still lightly rests
upon his wand.

Put up your instruments
the concert's over
the lights are going out
the sounds fade into memory
to rise again
but later
much much later...
the darkness fogs me round
I cannot find a road
to home.

II

Morning

Hanging in
learning my hurt
while you grow
glow worms
through our mutual night

Hanging in
dawn now
my new birth
breaching; its cords
hanging hope

Morning
my tenuous yellow
let eyes light
and shine me
to growth again.

FLY

ef a ketch im
a mash im
ef a ketch im
a mash im
ef a ketch im...

Will you walk into my parlour
Said the spider to the fly
It's the prettiest snugliest parlour
That ever you did spy...
And I
the fly
inspecting your web
this skein now then that
put my
microscope eye
through its intricate weave
saw valleys of cloud
blue and serene
saw acres of grass
sheltered and green.
Ephemeral and light
I rested my life
and dazzled
I watched
you wove me inside
and dazzled
I slept
my crysalis sleep...

* * *

I woke up inside
no more dazzled and green.
Awake and alert
unfolding my wings
I stretched...
But your skeins
not delicate now
resistant and strong
they wove me inside
I am trapped
I can't move
I can't butterfly
fly...

And you
perched outside
your eyes large and clear
you see acres of green
you see valleys of cloud
you can move
you can fly...
Now I look through the web
I look into the void
I see numberless flies
training microscope eyes
through intricate weave
ANANSI I cry
ANANSI-SI-SI I hear
the sky is too vast
how it scatters my cry
the sky is too clear
it hides my despair
they can't hear
they can't see
with their microscope eye...

ef a ketch im
a mash im
ef a ketch im
a mash im

A ketch im... im... im

AFTER CAGES

Behind remembered Sunday papers
sits my father's grunts
rain patter or the sharp uneven crunch
of children's feet toeing the gravel
Mulvina's off again (I hear her say)...
Did you remember, called your mother yesterday?...
and chews more firmly on his latest pipe.

After the patter
after children's tired toes
the silent Sunday
thunders this bird's exit
leaving her window-peering silent
newly old.

Someday I'd say
she'll up and go
leaving him window-peering under rain
drops chewing pipes
at home
no going when it's no one that you are leaving.

Behind these Sunday papers
sits my father's silence now
hearkening the raindrops' patter
or the pebbles empty of remembered feet;
parsley and mint fragrant where I remember
brown pipes and brown tobacco littering the ash

Soundless we sit
silent and impotent
who is Mulvina?
where his mother now?
I know no questions
feel no urge to learn
too late I know
he needs to answer
lonely women newly old
but oddly silenced now
stretched out beside the flowers
boxed brown in aged mahogany.

ANANSA

IM no PERCEPT
how ABLE-Y
Anansa weaves
the only web she knows
around my house
(and not because
the house is mine)
she weaves because she must
the urge to weave comes in...
my house as if on wheels
goes out...

Anansa's threads are thin
and strong
so thin I can't perceive (nor he)
until I feel my house begin to move
pulled off, destabilised
by threads of magic web

He's on his hupentery
deep inside his desk
his space is changeless
till (and after many thoughts)
he steps outside...

the wind already cold
the neighbours gone beyond return
a new environ-
ment to blow his mind...

Empire fragments
in marble as in men.
The marble reconnects
but humpty dumpty's
fragments cannot hold.

The king tiif, the governor tiif
me tiif, you tiif, all a we tiif.
The king is forever a woman.

MARTHA

Woman desist
he cannot hear your flesh
your tongue and well-springs
over-elocute
her spirit speaks.

He tunes you out
but swings you in
with habit thrust
another she infuses all his sense
whose spirit throbs
and blows his body
in your mind
woman desist
and live.

DEJA VUE
(for DEEP)

there near that shattered stone
now hardly fit for two
silence and moonscape
touched our tenderness

later
that dream grew
silence slept
and voices rising
steps their vague
pat-patter
children
like fresh plants sprung
like flowers glowing
wildly from our earth

an end-
less time
and yet you kept me comfort
with your
soon
these times will be
like dots on our remembering
calmness come over all

now near that stone again
moonscape and silence
voices and footfall
mimic our memory

silence
now dreamless
that dream grew rich
to fill our silence
with its bounty.

if there were space enough
to hold our different lives
within one love
if there were myriad golden rings
molded into our ceremony...

so leaving you
I took the ring
savoured its smoothness
fingering its face
until my frightened nail
released its secret catch
snapped wide its circle
there
a clover
FIVE leafed
perfect
sprang
mirabile. I crossed myself
and whispering trembling thanks
I snapped it close.

SCREWS LOOSE

I do not wish to sit and smile
too sweetly where the pavement ends
nor set small windy fires at Papine
nor scrupulously cleanse myself in streams
guttering too slowly
gathering stench on stench

I do not wish to mumble as I go
gesturing wildly as the voice grows old
eyes staring wide
and crude uneasy laugh

mad people whisper late
sane people's early dreams
beware my inmost thoughts
that wait mad mind's release

too much too soon
the mind rejects it all
uncensored now and overflowing here
flotsam and jetsam mixed with precious pearl

and so my love my seraph dear go home
mad women whisper sane men's names
and not in jest
leave me my dreams of growing calmly old
turning thin pages in moth-ridden books
rocking my evening bones
watching each sun go down

vaiván
vaiván
the funeral dance
the woman hears
her soul's own moan
no drums
no fifes
no shak-shaks tell
her feet
the inner rhythm's
beat
hand on her head
cloth tight on her belly
vaiván
vaiván
soliloquent steps
lovely the tune
lonely the grief

    madda Balla
    tie yu belly
    Sammy dead...O
    Sammy dead
    Sammy dead
    Sammy dead...O

the harvest dance
the woman must dance
to the potent beat
of the family drums
to the rattle of gourd
to the whistle of fife

she must dance
with the women
dance
to the men
pattern of hand
of hip of foot

    for your song is my song
    and my song is your song
    the more we sing together
    the happier we shall be

Sometimes to company
sometimes to peace
o fast alone the spirit
surfeiting
with too much comfort
too much intercourse

    vaiván
    vaiván
    the woman hears
    her sweet soul's moan
    Sammy dead...O

Guardian of the Great Tradition
those volumes stood
in sturdy black
and through their golden teeth of leaves
sent whispers down:
pass gently gently
touch me not
touch me not for I am holy

Guardian of a great tradition
those statues stood
remembering Egypt
and from the stone lips of the sphinx
the silent whisper
touch me not
and pass me gently
I am cold and I am lonely
I am freezing naked poorly
for I need the golden desert
need its parching on my stone

From the hollow of that sound
from the screaming of that rape
to the shelter of my nothing...

Then the voice of that other
took my hand in his invisible hand
and led me to the bed of the river
where little banks like dunes of sand
sit waterless in the river's lap
and over my head his inaudible voice:

this is the voice of the waterless river
this is the voice of the shallow peaks
these are the books of endless unbinding...

And the voice of his hand
held my hand firm and led me
to my timeless children
who played in their present
Tannique and Tungi
Kamau and Abenna

Show them your river
said his soundless voice
show them the dunes
the dry sanded bank-heads
the clear mountain trickle
that tomorrow will fall
white foam falls of beauty
let them play in this present
where the grass greens low
and the silt land is ready

And these books of endless unbinding
will fatten with the leaves of their reaping
and the seamless wide open wall sides
will green with the pages of their toil...
tomorrow belongs to the children.

REMEMBERING WASHINGTON DC

In Washington
Black DC
not to be confused with
Washington White DC
one Sunday
I saw God

Yes I saw God
in clothes He wouldn't recognise
in every habit man has ever worn
I saw Him ageing bald
with three piece suit bow tie
I saw Him robed in purple black and brown
and then I saw Hun beating Babylon down
strutting and young
and under flowing gown
complete with fez to crown
His black hamitic face

and He got poorer
as His clothes got looser
until He sat on stoops
and rapped with sisters
smelling of incense
blackness and conversion
where Florida merged with
Georgia on my mind (?)

Sunday
down Florida

I knew
Black folks have God
White folks have

at least
in Washington
DC

BITTERLAND

Listening your tale
tells me how woman I have felt for girls
fighting with wigs and powder caught strap-
hanging in the galleys of the USA

you tell me your New York
your Brooklyn and the Bronx
your island childhood cut in half
too soon a man
and all that little-understood
no longer folks
but black folks
hacks up there
where eyes forget to smile
and learn to bare unwilling
teeth in greeting (?)

the scars like keloids
mark the back of your remembering
like pictures shot too sharp
grow large in retrospect

A thousand spades
a thousand journeys
each generation's new roots
grown in air
or barely touching ground
twisted and gnarled...

Unless like yours
their luck
was in.

FOREIGN

Documentary
from Korea
fascinating Guyana
Mass games... or mask
frightening ayah

I saw it again in Havana
that first night of CARIFESTA
and thought now
Why am I
scared by screens
not moved
like everybody clapping?

these screens are children

little school ones
in their uniforms
with paper squares
without their faces

a people screen
fine backdrop for the feat
of poet
playwright
politician
friend

the screen is children nowhere is a child

In America they make composites
They make composites of criminals
(does criminal = black?)

and I ask
Why not
photographs or words
like in the country
I come from?

In America
when people stop me
(people meaning white)
it's not me
it's just the last black
model
dancer
addict
they've not known
In America I am faceless
other people's
versions of myself
not me

And now I know
why I fear
Mass Games
Screens
Black people without faces...
and Composites

LOS ANGELES

and what if angels
remembering flat roofs and long-skirted nuns
descend to sit here and to cast their eyes
towards the clouds gliding like listless sheep
across the evening sky

rooftops rise here too high now
cars rush loud
and grey smog hangs below the clouds
low visibility
no silence now
nor any peace

Angels would bash their trusting faces in descent
and loud trucks groaning under garbage
harvest up their wings
and altar boys no longer beautiful and brown
white now with angel dust
would loudly laugh at broken angel faces
dirty now
city lost angeles

and yet the purple jacaranda
blooms and dies
in beauty
(like my yellow poui)
along the green.

FROM MANDAHL PEAK

I

One brown free islet
humped like a turtle
looks out upon
one flawless blue-grey
line touching the sky

looks sadly out
considering islands
far less free
that gaze on that
same flawless line...

Blue-grey
(with green nearer the land)
calm and impenetrable
the sea
smiles with unparted lips

and one small daring skiff
streaks on its surface
leaving a trail of white
foaming to who knows where
sea-floor or shore.

Noon

This oasis is brown
the sea is green desert
round the islet
rising like a whale
giant with tears
streaming her sullen chin

my friend she sighs
is dead
for death 'is not
the undiscovered country
death is here'

This islet rises silent
saying you can't kill me...
hurts with pity
for the sister hillsides
visible from there
scarred now with condominiums
white like race
for sea front
restless like the boats
that jostle huge ships
white again like race

better sit naked
silent in your peace
than clothed in stars (and stripes)
and decked with beauty
worn like clothes too tight
and man like dog eat dog

Night

The islet now lies lost
lies sleeping shrouded
by grey cloud grey sea

and fallen stars
light up the stolen hillsides
of the sister isle
diamonds and sapphires
of the US eye

till morning shuts the eyes of stars
returning hillsides to their scars.

BELIZE SUITE

I: *Sea Wall*

Only a gentle swish
Where waves would touch the land
no wind no turbulence
along this wall arranged by man
dividing land from sea

No cruise-ships light this harbour end
to end only that cluster
where the army lights
ride there at anchor...
cool darkness and deluding calm

houses sit silent near the water's edge
their calm precarious like our peace
hoisted on stilts
like mokojumbies in the carnival
listening the ocean's gentle murmur
hearing its angry wail
what seems like decades now
when death rode loud and furious
on the hissing waves

From storm and earthquake Lord
deliver us
and us
and us

II: *Xunantunich*
(for Roy W)

The gods will ask
tell them I left my offering there
three handspans to the left
of that dread corner where the two slabs meet
under a stone
set in a threadbag
that I kept between my breasts
so that my hands could help me
timid goat
climb halfway up
no more

it isn't strength that matters
courage to climb
is what the old hearts lose
my children's children never now will know
what sights the high-priests saw
undizzied by the dizzying heights

Power is always from on high
lookouts where pirates guard the harbour
rivers that tumble down from angry hills
cloud tops for cherubim
and Maya priests' Xunantunich

III: *Road from Xunantunich*

Dusk settles in
first near the edge
where towns like pale mirages sit
and only slowly shrouds us
shocked to silence by the stillness here...

Where are the night sounds
that begin at dusk?
not here or just not yet?

King trees with long and hairless trunks
reach green and fertile locks
towards the sky

no mountains here no rocks
no green between those thick locks
and the close cropped kinks
that can't protect the land
cracked now with long unsightly breaks
(the geolog unstraps his EYE and clicks)

Who would be king
but with no subjects
who would grow strong and perfect
but alone?

This silence sobers us
and sends us feverish
seeking home

IMPRESSIONS – HAVANA 1979

I

And what is there to see
so long after the last of the marines
the last of modish cars
the last of fashionable dames
liquid with moonlit glasses
or sequined underneath harsh lights
and urgent hands?

It is an empty city
clean streets where many lanes
lie mocking swift pedestrian feet
that follow glances upstreet and downstreet
expectantly

but no cars come
large overcrowded buses
hurry workers tired
to their dormitories
as evening settles in

and bright lights now
no longer usher in the night.

II

It was Manhattan
          without the cars
It was Madrid
          without the bull-ring
and so perhaps
I felt a body vacant
waiting for its animus

this city that Espana must have loved
to mark her image here tan cuidosamente
where Yankis must have drunk delight
so deep
that they would wish
to recreate their citadel
their Casa Blanca
near this perfect sea

But I want to celebrate
the animus this city waits
now springing
sweet and slender
clear-eyed
children

for I have listened to them work in learning centres
and I have watched them playing in the squares
and they have made me listen in the streets
almost as if they knew
that I would want to sense
their budding...

Tomorrow I will visit Havana again
when the spirit full-blown
inhabits the city
and I will hear the city talk
and I will forget Manhattan
I will forget Madrid
I will hear Havana... de Cuba.

III

The great mulatto nation disappears
after the belch of the tunnel
al avenida del puerto

Aquí in old Havana
little blacks
our old men toothless
smiling solidarity...verdad
our children
none too clean
flooding the plazas
near the cathedral
God once called his own
the children
none too clean
but fed...verdad
and thank God
smiling confidence

We have become accustomed to finding us
in the kitchens of large cities
we have become accustomed to finding us
on the docks of large cities

and so these old men
smiling toothless
nodding memories
of seas they sailed
old salts
watching their grandsons
tumble near the flagstones
don't surprise us here

allà in my Jamaica
street-light children
scrounge 'beg you a ten cents nuh'
black angels
hungry angels

these angels here
they smile
they eat
they play
their good abuelos
toothless sit
but smile.

BIMSH

foam fans lie white against the sand
cottages like cartons newly neatly stacked
show pink against the blue...
descent begins
in row on row of white on black
policemen polish up their act
left right left right
inaudible from here

the engine gently purrs
a slight airpocket
and Grantley Adams (with Seawell
printed here and there)
receives the shudder
gentle
of the DC9

ERNIE
(For Hazel)

At Rudy's
after twelve
he trumpets old notes
sweet notes

white folks with throaty giggles
crinkle-pink with too much music
too much alcohol
retiring pleased to rooms uptown
in swank hotels
smile Ernie dollars

black folks smile smiles and so
I sip
another daiquiri
to float me near each lover
whisked from yesteryear
and filtered through
the muted O

lovers who danced
lovers who counter-rhymed
my fledgling verse
and lovers who sat earnestly
while other hornmen
blew such sweetness
as this Ernie
blows here free
and freely from his horn

at Rudy's
after twelve

ROSEAU AUGUST '79

I had wished for water
to call my city to its baptism
or earthquake
to possess it to rebirth

But today I watch your city
clean and fresh
baptiscd with water
and with wind
like the beginning
after chaos fled

and I confess
that like you
I walk in agony
longing for dirt and sin
or pre-baptismal stench
for something/anything

this pure clean nothing
shatters me and yet
who knows
tomorrow's city its rebirth
what shape
tomorrow with its dark unknown
unnerves us

I had wished for my city's baptism
but today I rejoice in my city
and share your tears
that yours has grown so clean.

RAIN FOREST

Behind
red water kriki black mixed with red
ahead
dirt narrow trails like forest streets
named for their trees bruinhart and groen
those trees...
(men here are ten feet tall)
with hairless trunks
and large protecting leaves

without a change of air the rain comes in
strumming the leaves with strange unearthly tunes
and yet the trails stretch dry
rain breaks the silence hanging thick
and woodsmell mixes with the rain

     and now the call response of argument
     slices the one continuous strum with
     will you wont you will you
     wont...

Here in this forest power
Here with this raining glory
here finally we swear
to honour this great spirit love
taboo
bruinhart and groen and naked palm
bear strong and silent witness

BM REVISITED

'...the head of the Lapith is in the Louvre
and that of the Centaur in Athens...'
        (British Museum inscription)*

these fragments... how many spaces how many holes
how headless must a greek his culture sell
how threadless must he string
from Athens and the Louvre
to hulks of shapely beasts
their erstwhile heads
displaced where the imperial
master minds insist on London as the centre...

at home
this woman sir, her great grandfather was ashanti
that man his great was han chinese
uttar pradesh nurtured this great grandma
and here the randy irish/english sired

empire fragments
in marble as in men

But here a patchwork quilt
a vase from shards of ornate china
aged in tier on tier of household waste
folk dances where the afro rhythms
answer euro names (quadrille, schottische.)
our hodgepodge wholes
a finer axis now on which to turn
a place where to begin
a better centre...

**the head of the Lapith is on the trunk of the Centaur*

LONG MOUNTAIN
(Travelogue for Rooftops and George R)

I

too young
too new
too far
too future
books clutter my spaces
Long Mountain shoulder
shelter me
plodding
this innocent beat
to your warm open hill-door

II

white
bright
coldlight fresh snow-
flakes printless
waiting footfall
waiting ploughfall
this land breeds tyrants
Long Mountain shoulder
show me your green mind
melting this lovelessness

III

Manhattan brick
on claustro-
phobic
brick
thrown up
near sky
line
underground rumblings
black tikki tikki
white tikki tikki
dock in their destiny
Long Mountain shoulder
hug close my psyche

IV

roads rush to river
roads rush to sea-
wall canals to koker
swamps swell this land
spaced mudtide to landedge
cottages crawl
horizon hunting
watch where their fathers
hunted your fathers
hiding
hoping
endless this openness
fitted you fatalist...
maronage mock me
Long Mountain shoulder
hide me in history
maronage make me

V

maronage waiting
Long Mountain hold me
leaning this shudder
quaked on your shoulder
pine green above me
pine smell all over me
mist and the morning
mend this cracked spirit
fit firm this wild mind
splintered with wandering
Long Mountain hug me
hushed on your shoulder
maronage shelter me
maronage make me

AUTUMN LEAVES

Now autumn leaves
wait no September
yellowing my window
breaking the night-
hush

wait no September
friends
falling
early

and children
clutching time-cards
open earth
gently
the doors of earth
as if their little hands
hold measures
equal Methuselah's
wait no September

Cracking the unhatched egg
under the hen's damp wing
fading the urgent bud
before its flowering
breaking the slender twig
before its hardening
I only come, smiles Death,
when evening falls...

My measure measures evening
yours with innocence conceived
tests not nor knows
the taste of nectar
from the rose so soon
the touch of feathers
formed within the shell
the turn of twig
mature before its time.
Only my measure
checks the guango's trunk
and checks the rose
its petals bending
at the fevered day.
Only my measure knows.

LINES IN SORROW
(for the Adams)

another young one gone
another mother sighs
cho! all this fuss
making them fit to earn
the living we don't know
that they will ever need
them dying off like
Kingston butterflies

one time
I too had said
that I would stop and wait
and wait to go
since that must come
but the cynic I was living with said
people like you promise to die young
then hang on here forever
living off the rest

that way it didn't sound
too wise

It's the perhaps
that threatens.

FOR 'TIME'
Oct. 18, 1976

Tonight my love
the drums are cold
and drum-sticks sickly
lean about the corner
where my father
warmed his ageing skin
or fed his eyesight
on the city sprawling
underneath our hill

the drums are cold;
went cold beneath my hands
the moment that his spirit fled;
spoke nothing mindless of our care
and mindless of the white libations
sprinkled from my lips...

the drums will speak again
tomorrow when his body underearths;
the drums must speed him
home outside that other hill
that looks over our valley
and the sea

and afterwards
these drums will only speak
beyond tomorrow
when his children
live my father's dreams
beyond the time
when fires flaming on his land
blacken what must burn out
to burst another better
living for my father's seed

then drums my love
will sweeten all this hill
and hark my father's spirit
home from fruitless wanderings
to sit beside its pulse
and hear my children sing
and watch their fingers
speak these very drums he loved
then joy my father's shade.

REMEMBERING
(for Adlith)

Pearldrops she said
and pointed towards her breasts...
too cold for turning on, I said
my poets warm to raisins tipping
naseberries on the limb

pearldrops are cold and white
and dead
how ever came that image in your head?

now that the doctors say
the end is on its way
I find me thinking... pearldrops...
Pre-suggesting...

'pearls lie deep'
the ocean
gathering lifedrops
storing on its floor
cold people with cold pearls

Pearldrops
I hear her say
and note (too late)
the wanness of her voice.

FAREWELL
(to Adlith)

It is the moonlight
glinting at the frilled cloud's edge
that marks your passing

this moon's full turn
that marks its end
and marks too the beginning
of yet another moon
brief now and bright
its full four phases done

and these our lives
concentric circles
etched out each in each
He sees them equal

He sets a ladder
reaching to the skies
and gently pulls a tread
releasing you or me

while other trodders watch
and silent wonder
Lord whose tread is next?

REVELATION
(From Doris)

Frailty thy name is...
body struggle-ing to reach
one final breath taking
angry quakes wracking
body belieing
the you calmly dying

amen
amen
amen
Into thy hands we deliver
this spirit

What mighty struggle this to leave
was there an equal struggle to arrive?

We miss each time
the foetus fighting
to become a child
the urgent forcing to perceive the world
all our concern poised loving
on the bearer blooming
mother hurting...

that early breath outside the careful womb
that cry of life as Naana slaps the guest
is surely mother to this stifling breath

amen
amen
amen
pass me the pennies for her eyes

TWO FOR NEVILLE

I

The fisherman closes his net
the sailor is home from the sea
good night Jim
good night Jack
good night Josefina

If you go home
don't ask for me
or anyone
Just wait and read each morning's
In Memoriam
where every column
prints
some keen fresh face
you only think of on a bicycle
grinning like mad
in one dimension

Old age
is not the sitting and recounting tales
is not the leisure to enjoy your friends
They lied who spoke of endless sunsets
And they knew better
they had lived the wars
and those familiar suitcases
sent back as
luggage unaccompanied

Learn how the moving finger writes...
these lessons come too quick and sharp
to our unreadiness
life is a river only because

so many little streams
touch end to end

What gives it meaning?
that's the philosopher's trip
and whether he gazes on a stone
or a lightbulb
or a peeny-wally
There's nothing he will know
unless the Great Mind
takes him in His trust
shows him the masterplan
so large
so comprehensive
he won't understand
and so he still won't know

No one philosophy can answer all
each man is an island
each mind is a muffin tin a
and so we sit with our invisible pencils
working out strategies
to cope with brevity
to cope with our adieux
to love – too sweet to forget
to life – too intense to leave
but most
to friends and friendships
mangroves of our shelter
stuck with benches everywhere
saying
'now tell me...'

The man was ready
he had his Jerusalem Bible
marked off at a page
warning us to be ready
every yesterday

And because he was an artist
it's the psalmist's word he took
'My days (are) listed and determined
even before the first of them occurred'

Awareness is all
Something had touched him
some event
had put him on a thought path
few suspect.
Unlikely...

Every Sunday
shirtsleeves and tie
the weekday jeansman
reading the lesson
passing the velvet bag
and 'peace be unto you
and you
and you'

Peace be unto you
my friend and brother
for I-ver

SU SU

Susu su su   Susu su su
among the yellow poui
you hear
I hear
leaves in the Japanese garden
'tiday fi mi tumaro fi yu'
like Brer Anancy talking in his nose
Susu su su

And how I laughed that day
I heard them say
'im shouldn bury there
im a go come back fi dem have no fear'
denying all the rural wisdom I had known...

Then quick and fast
some hidden hit man
strikes us off our anxious lists
and you
and I
stand open-mouthed
as poui leaves whisperjust before they fall

tiday fi mi
tumaro fi yu
Susu su su
Susu su su

OUR MOTHER
(for Lixie)

'Strew on her roses roses
And never a touch of yew...'

Orange and red for our mother
who sang us bright songs...
jigging from side to side
pointing her index fingers
doing the Bustamante
the K-walk ('Cake' they correct me now)
and tuned (perhaps an octave high)
that 'you can't hinder me
from loving you...'

who stored long poems
neatly script
in her best blackboard hand
and fancy scrap books
weddings full
used press books
pasted over
pop songs
fit for a younger queen (?)
'Butterflies green butterflies blue
Oh how they flutter up and butter up for you...'
and mixed the ages endlessly
flowing each generation into each
'South of the border
dont mestik away...'
(I couldnt figure that
till I could read
and scrap-book settled it
'down Mexico way')

then I saw
broad black hats
and squat young yellow men
winking their eyes
in lies
saying manana...

No tears
no sad songs
for our lady
who jigged from this life
into that
and did not wave adieu...

Endless and timeless
rediscoveries
headfuls of history
voicefuls of song
duets and trios
moonshine and mystery...
watch di moonshine baby man
still sitting there in the morning

and hid her hardships
underneath the fictive griefs
of Lucy Gray, Lord Ullin's child,
Mary Maguire
who stole three loaves
and drove the judge to tears...
all suffering whites
she didnt know nor cared
or else conveniently forgot
insisting still
unquestioned Coromanti
and did not live to have them tell her
she was not.

TO GRAN... AND NO FAREWELL

I didnt wish to see the moth-marks
where your Khus Khus smelled
the high weeds crowding the forget-me-nots
or alien fingers
handling knives and spoons
kept sheening in brown calico

and so I let the years
make jumbie chain-links
ages long
before I brought
bright florets for your grave

One room remains
and one small fretwork shard
among the rotted beams
ingrown with baby grass
remembers still the august Entry Hall
tributes of broken china
lean-to tables
and an old man
shambling out and in
cursing the vultures
who would snatch the land...

I round the corner
eager with my shrubs
the grave at last...
then unbelieving shudder
Corpie's tomb
Naomi's garden square
and yours that now
my mind will never hold

no single adoration
no peculiar tears
some well-intentioned
madman with his spade...
all now one vast sepulchraic mass

I crush the shrublets
tramp them underfoot
and with a heart
too swollen now for tears
descend the slope
without adieu.

Also by Velma Pollard
SHAME TREES DON'T GROW HERE

A shame tree is a Jamaican symbol for the development of moral consciousness, and the poems in this collection explore the points at which moral values emerge - and the consequences of their absence. The poems suggest toughly that such consciousness does not grow without unremitting effort and scrupulous sensitivity to feeling, but there is nothing didactic or moralistic about them. They are imaginative recreations of the dramas of coming to consciousness and the inevitable ambiguities of truth. As in all Velma Pollard's work, there is a deeply imbued sense of Caribbean history.

Marvin Williams writes in *The Caribbean Writer*: 'Tone and emotion range wider in Velma Pollard's *Shame Trees Don't Grow Here... but poincianas bloom* - from disgust, anger, and outrage to celebration, awe, and praise; from questioning and condemnation to understanding and reconciliation. The major thrust of the poet's fire comes in the first part of the book where those who lacked or are lacking conscience and moral boundaries are drawn into Pollard's unflinching scrutiny. Wildfire becomes hearth in part two where the beauty and life-enhancing qualities of land, sea, and people are celebrated. Throughout, the poet's skillful use of language remains evident in, for example, her subtle, unobtrusive rhymes that lend musicality to her verse; her puns; double entendres; and other word play.'

ISBN: 0-948833-48-3
Price: £6.99
Pages: 72
Published: February 1993

Peepal Tree Press publishes a wide selection of outstanding fiction, poetry, drama, history and literary criticism with a focus on the Caribbean, Africa, the South Asian diaspora and Black life in Britain. Peepal Tree is now the largest independent publisher of Caribbean writing in the world. All our books are high quality original paperbacks designed to stand the test of time and repeated readings.

All Peepal Tree books should be available through your local bookseller, though you are even more welcome to place orders direct with us on the Peepal Tree website and on-line bookstore: www.peepaltreepress.com. You can also order direct by phone or in writing.

Peepal Tree sends out regular e-mail information about new books and special offers. We also produce a yearly catalogue which gives current prices in sterling, US and Canadian dollars and full details of all our books. Contact us to join our mailing list.

You can contact Peepal Tree at:

17 King's Avenue
Leeds LS6 1QS
United Kingdom

e-mail hannah@peepalpeepaltreepress.com
tel: 44 (0)113 245 1703

website: www.peepaltreepress.com